MILITARY AIRCRAFT

F/A-18E/F
SUPER HORNET

BY DONNA MCKINNEY

TORQUE™

BELLWETHER MEDIA · MINNEAPOLIS, MN

Torque brims with excitement perfect for thrill-seekers of all kinds. Discover daring survival skills, explore uncharted worlds, and marvel at mighty engines and extreme sports. In *Torque* books, anything can happen. Are you ready?

This edition first published in 2024 by Bellwether Media, Inc.

No part of this publication may be reproduced in whole or in part without written permission of the publisher. For information regarding permission, write to Bellwether Media, Inc., Attention: Permissions Department, 6012 Blue Circle Drive, Minnetonka, MN 55343.

Library of Congress Cataloging-in-Publication Data

Names: McKinney, Donna B. (Donna Bowen), author.
Title: F/A-18E/F Super Hornet / by Donna McKinney.
Description: Minneapolis, MN : Bellwether Media, Inc., 2024. |
Series: Torque: Military Aircraft | Includes bibliographical references and index. | Audience: Ages 7-12 | Audience: Grades 4-6 |
Summary: "Engaging images accompany information about the F/A-18E/F Super Hornet. The combination of high-interest subject matter and light text is intended for students in grades 3 through 7"– Provided by publisher.
Identifiers: LCCN 2023046959 (print) | LCCN 2023046960 (ebook) | ISBN 9798886878189 (library binding) | ISBN 9798886879124 (ebook)
Subjects: LCSH: Hornet (Jet fighter plane)–Juvenile literature.
Classification: LCC UG1242.F5 M 3977 2024 (print) | LCC UG1242.F5 (ebook) | DDC 623.74/63–dc23/eng/20231012
LC record available at https://lccn.loc.gov/2023046959
LC ebook record available at https://lccn.loc.gov/2023046960

Text copyright © 2024 by Bellwether Media, Inc. TORQUE and associated logos are trademarks and/or registered trademarks of Bellwether Media, Inc.

Editor: Kieran Downs   Designer: Jeffrey Kollock

Printed in the United States of America, North Mankato, MN.

TABLE OF CONTENTS

TAKE-OFF AT SEA	4
WHAT IS THE F/A-18E/F SUPER HORNET?	6
BUILT FOR BATTLE	10
THE FUTURE OF THE SUPER HORNET	18
F/A-18E/F SUPER HORNET FACTS	20
GLOSSARY	22
TO LEARN MORE	23
INDEX	24

TAKE-OFF AT SEA

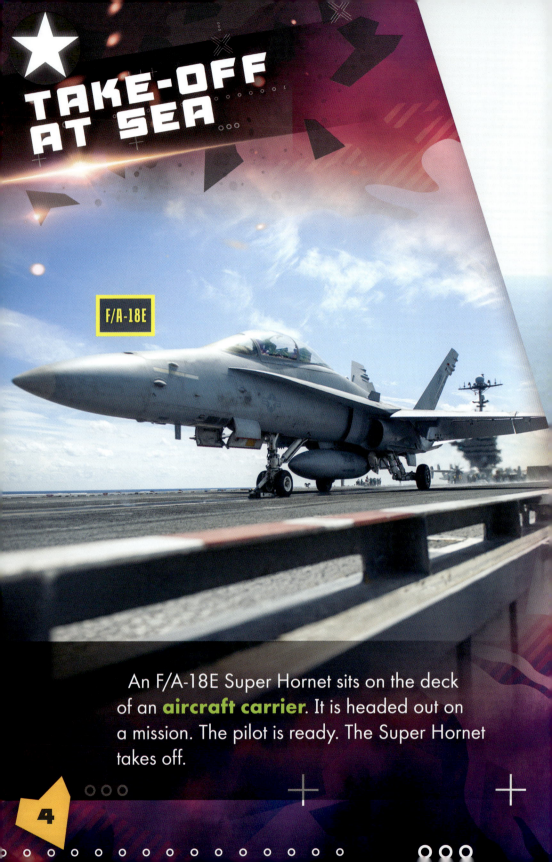

F/A-18E

An F/A-18E Super Hornet sits on the deck of an **aircraft carrier**. It is headed out on a mission. The pilot is ready. The Super Hornet takes off.

4

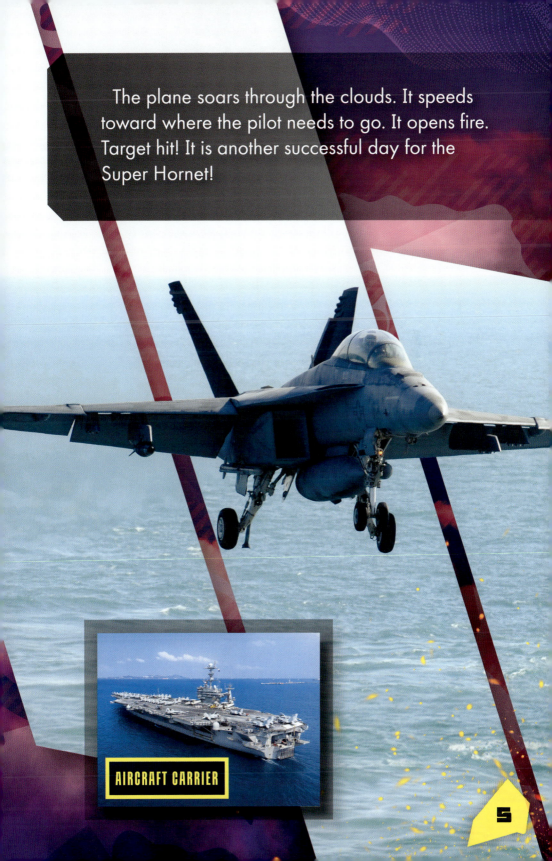

The plane soars through the clouds. It speeds toward where the pilot needs to go. It opens fire. Target hit! It is another successful day for the Super Hornet!

AIRCRAFT CARRIER

WHAT IS THE F/A-18E/F SUPER HORNET?

The Super Hornet is a United States Navy aircraft. It is both an attack and a fighter aircraft. It battles enemy aircraft. It also battles enemy forces on the ground!

There are two models of the Super Hornet. They are the F/A-18E and the F/A-18F. Militaries in some other countries also have Super Hornets.

BLUE ANGELS

The Blue Angels are a Navy flight demonstration team. Since 2020, they have flown Super Hornets. They put on shows for the public to watch!

BLUE ANGELS SUPER HORNET

The U.S. Navy began using the F/A-18E/F Super Hornet in 1999. It was a newer version of the F/A-18 Hornet.

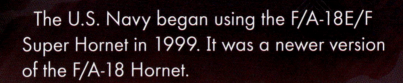

OPERATION SOUTHERN WATCH
SUPER HORNET ON USS *ABRAHAM LINCOLN*

The Super Hornet is mainly used in **combat** missions. Its first mission was Operation Southern Watch. It happened in Iraq in 2002. Later, it was a part of Operation Enduring Freedom. It also flew during Operation Iraqi Freedom.

MISSIONS MAP

Operation Southern Watch	Iraq, 2002
Operation Iraqi Freedom	Iraq, 2003 to 2011
Operation Odyssey Dawn	Libya, 2011
Operation Enduring Freedom	Afghanistan, 2001 to 2014

BUILT FOR BATTLE

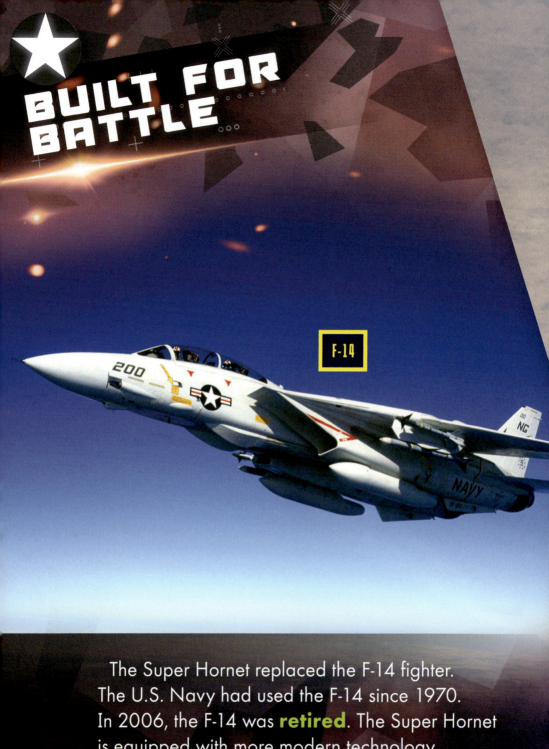

F-14

The Super Hornet replaced the F-14 fighter. The U.S. Navy had used the F-14 since 1970. In 2006, the F-14 was **retired**. The Super Hornet is equipped with more modern technology.

The F/A-18E Super Hornet has a single seat for one pilot. The F/A-18F **cockpit** has two seats. They are for a pilot and a **weapons system officer**.

COCKPIT

WEAPONS SYSTEM OFFICER

F/A-18F

PILOT

TOP GUN

The Super Hornet appeared in the 2022 movie *Top Gun: Maverick*.

The Super Hornet carries weapons for fighting enemies in the air and on the ground. Some of its weapons are "smart" weapons. These bombs and **missiles** are guided by computers.

PARTS OF AN F/A-18F SUPER HORNET

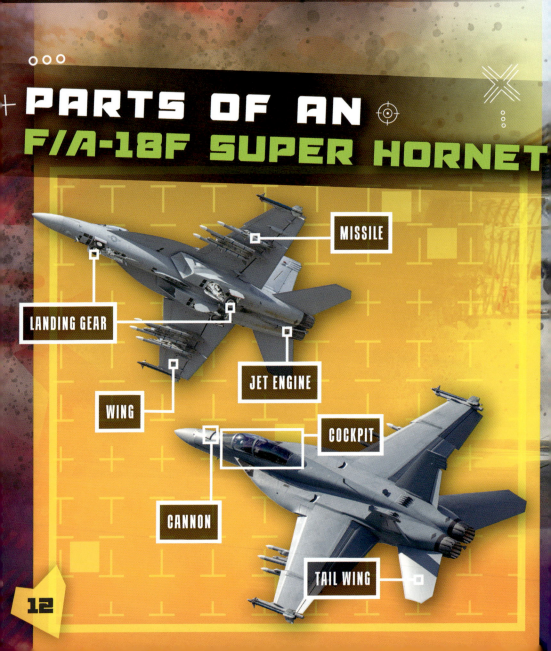

- MISSILE
- LANDING GEAR
- JET ENGINE
- WING
- COCKPIT
- CANNON
- TAIL WING

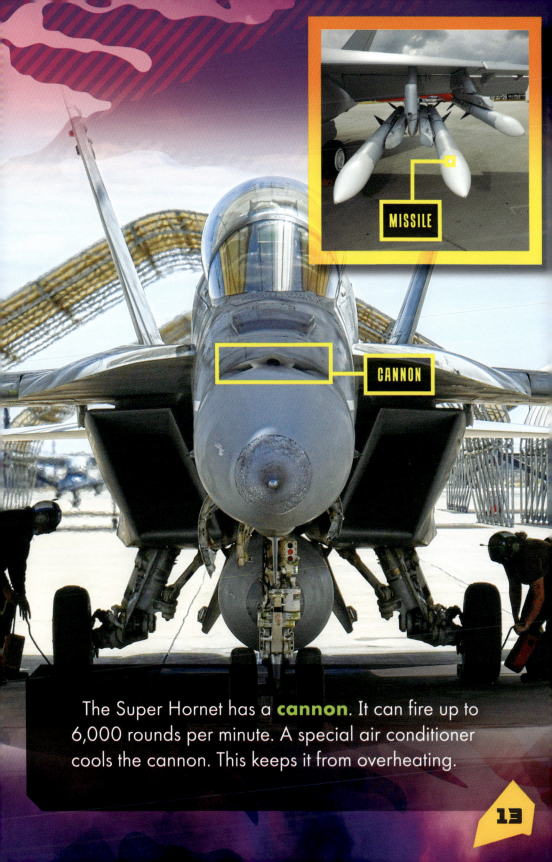

MISSILE

CANNON

The Super Hornet has a **cannon**. It can fire up to 6,000 rounds per minute. A special air conditioner cools the cannon. This keeps it from overheating.

The Super Hornet can take off and land on short runways. It can easily leave and land on an aircraft carrier!

CATAPULT

AIRCRAFT CARRIER CATAPULT

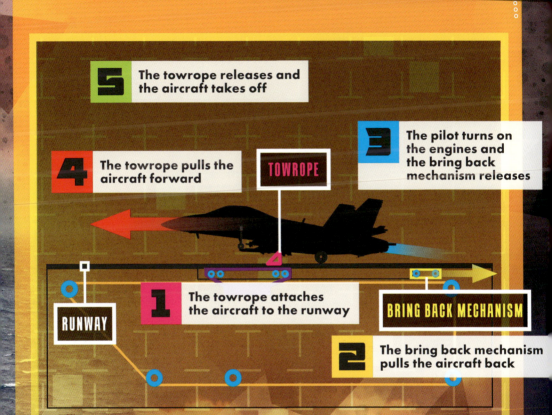

5 The towrope releases and the aircraft takes off

4 The towrope pulls the aircraft forward

3 The pilot turns on the engines and the bring back mechanism releases

TOWROPE

RUNWAY

1 The towrope attaches the aircraft to the runway

BRING BACK MECHANISM

2 The bring back mechanism pulls the aircraft back

The aircraft carrier has a **catapult**. It works like a slingshot. This helps the plane reach high speeds and quickly take off. Super Hornets use **tailhooks** to land. They hook onto **arresting wires** to slow the plane.

JET ENGINES

The Super Hornet has powerful jet engines. These help pilots quickly steer and fly. The plane can reach speeds up to 1,228 miles (1,976 kilometers) per hour.

SIZE CHART

LENGTH
60.3 FEET (18.4 METERS)

HEIGHT
16 FEET (4.87 METERS)

WIDTH AND WINGSPAN
44.9 FEET (13.68 METERS)

The Super Hornet has curved surfaces that are hard for enemy **radar** to detect. It has **stealth** coatings and high-tech radar. The Super Hornet has special lighting. It is hard for enemies to see it at night.

THE FUTURE OF THE SUPER HORNET

The Super Hornet is a powerful aircraft. It supports U.S. Navy missions in peacetime and war.

The U.S. Navy plans to stop building new Super Hornets in 2025. They plan to build F-35s instead. But they will continue to use the Super Hornet for years to come!

F-35

F/A-18E/F SUPER HORNET FACTS

STATS

TOP SPEED

1,218 miles
(1,960 kilometers)
per hour

RANGE

1,467 miles
(2,361 kilometers)

ALTITUDE CEILING

more than
50,000 feet
(15,240 meters)

MANUFACTURER

Boeing

BRANCH OF THE MILITARY

U.S. Navy

WEAPONS

UP TO **14** MISSILES

OR

UP TO **10** BOMBS

412 GATLING GUN ROUNDS

MAIN PURPOSE

combat

CLASS

MULTI-ROLE ATTACK AND FIGHTER AIRCRAFT

CREW

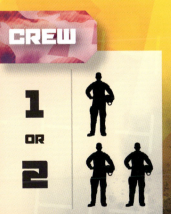

1 OR **2**

OPERATION

OVER **500** SUPER HORNETS IN USE TODAY

FIRST YEAR USED

1999

21

GLOSSARY

aircraft carrier—a large ship that allows aircraft to take off and land at sea

arresting wires—heavy wires stretched across the deck of an aircraft carrier to slow an aircraft that is landing

cannon—a large gun

catapult—a device that flings an object a great distance

cockpit—the part of an aircraft where the crew sits

combat—a fight between armed forces

missiles—explosives that are sent to targets

radar—a device that uses energy waves to sense and see objects

retired—no longer used

stealth—related to being designed to avoid being seen

tailhooks—hooks on the tails of some aircraft; the tailhook snags the arresting wires on the aircraft carrier deck to slow the aircraft when it is landing.

weapons systems officer—a person who manages the weapons on the Super Hornet and helps with navigation and communication

TO LEARN MORE

AT THE LIBRARY

Colson, Rob. *Awesome Aircraft*. New York, NY.: Enslow Publishing, 2023.

Hustad, Douglas. *US Navy: Equipment and Vehicles*. Minneapolis, Minn.: ABDO, 2022.

Noll, Elizabeth. *Stealth Technology*. Minneapolis, Minn.: Bellwether Media, 2022.

ON THE WEB

FACTSURFER

Factsurfer.com gives you a safe, fun way to find more information.

1. Go to www.factsurfer.com

2. Enter "F/A-18E/F Super Hornet" into the search box and click 🔍.

3. Select your book cover to see a list of related content.

INDEX

aircraft carrier, 4, 5, 14, 15
arresting wires, 15
Blue Angels, 7
bombs, 12
cannon, 13
catapult, 14, 15
coatings, 17
cockpit, 11
combat, 9
computers, 12
enemies, 6, 12, 17
F-14, 10
F-35s, 18
F/A-18 Hornet, 8
F/A-18E/F Super Hornet facts, 20–21
future, 18
history, 7, 8, 9, 10
Iraq, 9
jet engines, 16
lighting, 17
map, 9

missiles, 12, 13
missions, 4, 8, 9, 18
models, 4, 6, 11
parts of an F/A-18F Super Hornet, 12
pilot, 4, 5, 11, 16
radar, 17
runways, 14
size, 17
speeds, 5, 15, 16
tailhooks, 15
Top Gun: Maverick, 11
United States Navy, 6, 7, 8, 10, 18
weapons, 12, 13
weapons system officer, 11

The images in this book are reproduced through the courtesy of: Malaury Buis/ DVIDS, cover; Jared Mancuso/ DVIDS, p. 3; Ethan T Miller/ DVIDS, p. 4; Ryan McLearnon/ DVIDS, p. 5; GreenOak, p. 5 (inset); Daniel Gheesling/ DVIDS, p. 6; Cody Hendrix/ DVIDS, p. 7; PJF Millitary Collection/ Alamy, p. 8; Stocktrek Images, Inc./ Alamy, p. 10; Duncan Bevan/DVIDS, p. 11; NA/ DVIDS, p. 11 (cockpit); Ryan Fletcher, pp. 12 (bottom, top), 16, 19; Drew Verbis/ DVIDS, p. 13; Aviation Images Ltd/ Alamy, p. 13 (missiles); Yeongsik Im, p. 14 (catapult); Felix Castillo Reyes/ DVIDS, p. 14; Jake Spencer, p. 18; Andrew Harker, p. 20; Joshua P Card/ DVIDS, p. 23.

24